THE
PEOPLE
REMEMBER

For Abadai, Bahati, and Zuberi:
You are your ancestors' wildest dreams
—I.Z.

For my Beloved ancestors,
who imagined all that we could be,
and for them, I'll keep dreaming
—L.W.

Balzer + Bray is an imprint of HarperCollins Publishers.

The People Remember
Text copyright © 2021 by Ibi Zoboi
Illustrations copyright © 2021 by Loveis Wise
All rights reserved. Manufactured in China.
No part of this book may be used or reproduced in any manner whatsoever without written permission except
in the case of brief quotations embodied in critical articles and reviews. For information address HarperCollins
Children's Books, a division of HarperCollins Publishers, 195 Broadway, New York, NY 10007.
www.harpercollinschildrens.com

Library of Congress Control Number: 2020949333
ISBN 978-0-06-291564-1

The artist used Photoshop to create the digital illustrations for this book.
Typography by Dana Fritts
22 23 24 25 SCP 10 9 8 7 6 5 4 3 2
❖
First Edition

THE
PEOPLE
REMEMBER

BY
IBI ZOBOI

ILLUSTRATED BY
LOVEIS WISE

BALZER + BRAY
An Imprint of HarperCollins Publishers

The people remember
when it first happened.

It was on a day and on a night,
during a rainy season and a dry season,
while celebrating a wedding
and embracing a new baby,
while sending a loved one
into the arms of the ancestors,
and while welcoming a stranger
into the warmth of the village.

The people remember
that it first happened
during a time of war.

The Ashanti and the Fulani,
the Empire of Mali,

the Hausa and Ibo
as well as the Kongo,

the Yoruba and Akan,
the Empire of Songhai,

the Kingdom of Dahomey,
the Mende and the Fon

are where the people
used to call home.

While telling stories under the star-speckled sky
about memories of the ancestors
watching from way up high,

the people remember
that it was an uncle and a father,
a daughter and a cousin,
an entire family and a whole village
that vanished under that great big

African sun.

The chiefs and the kings,
the betrayers and traitors,
for gold, copper, and iron,
sold the people
in this time of war.

The people remember
the ropes that bound them

on wrists and ankles.
They walked to the shore
for days and nights
through tears and shouts.

The people remember
this was a time of war.

The men with the guns,
skin like a pale sun,
the men with the whips,
the men on the ships

watched the people
leave their land,
never to return
as their bare feet
left footprints in the sand.

There in the bellies
of rocking boats
they curled their bodies,
singing and praying
to faraway gods
who maybe, just maybe
could help them fly,
could help them float.

Some stayed; some jumped,
thinking that home
was somewhere deep
beneath the wide ocean,
and maybe, just maybe
she was their mother.

Mami Wata they called her.

They landed on the shores
of South Carolina and Virginia,
Hispaniola and Brazil.
Some met their new masters,
while others escaped toward the hills.

In search of freedom,
the Hausa and Fulani, Mende and Fon
found a common language,
a new word for home.

In the land of the free,
home of the brave,

if only this new god
was one who saves
the people from the fields
of cotton and sugarcane
under that great big

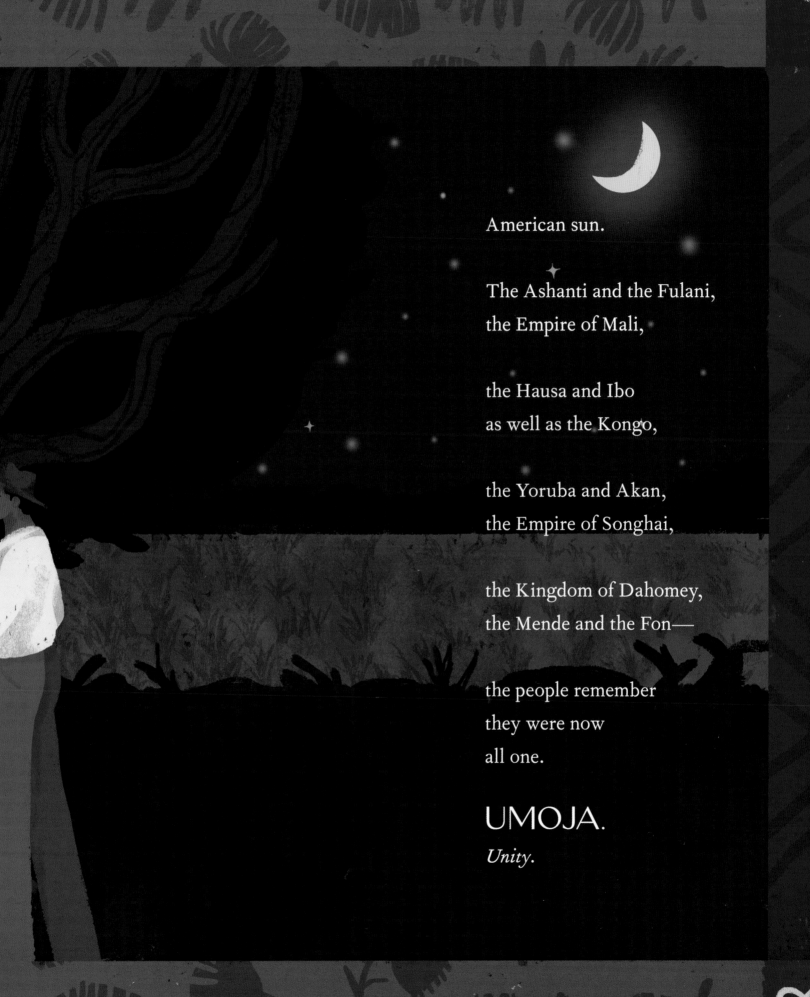

American sun.

The Ashanti and the Fulani,
the Empire of Mali,

the Hausa and Ibo
as well as the Kongo,

the Yoruba and Akan,
the Empire of Songhai,

the Kingdom of Dahomey,
the Mende and the Fon—

the people remember
they were now
all one.

UMOJA.

Unity.

∞

The people remember
when they did not have
their own bodies,
their own thoughts,
their own time.

When the days were long
and the sun was hot;

when the babies were born
and taken from their mothers;

when the sons left their families
and the fathers were sold away;

when the tears turned into rivers
and the shouts turned into music;

when the North Star was freedom
and Harriet Tubman led the way;

when Nat Turner demanded
that the people rise up;

when that other time of war
divided North from South—

the people fought
for land,
for freedom,
for a tomorrow
unknown.

The people remember
that like the rising and setting sun,
the winds turning from cool to warm,

they can change a time,
a today,
a tomorrow,
but never the past.

The people remember
that they have the power
to change this nation.

KUJICHAGULIA.

Self-determination.

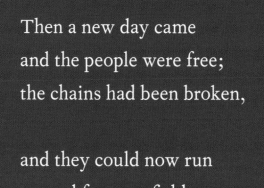

Then a new day came
and the people were free;
the chains had been broken,

and they could now run
toward faraway fields,
toward skies, toward sun,
toward each other,
toward lost ones,
and toward fathers and mothers.

From Mississippi to Chicago,
Georgia to New York,

from Alabama to California,
Louisiana to Canada,

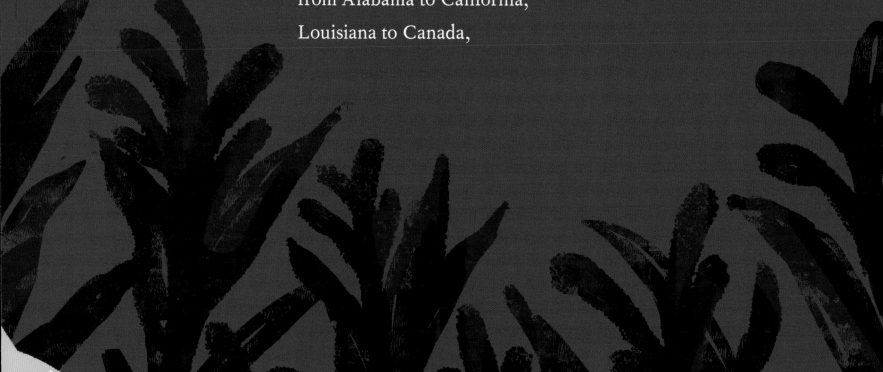

the people remember
that Great Migration
to new lands,
to new borders

where sharecropping hands
were now factory machine fingers.

The people toiled
and labored, working
the roads, the houses,
the skyscraping towers
reaching for that great big

American sun.

In the loud, bustling cities
and in the small, quiet towns,
the uncles and fathers,
daughters and cousins
gathered around a small table
and on a wide porch,
on a tattered couch
and on a vast green lawn,

to share jokes and stories,
tall tales and riddles,
to play the dozens
and jump the broom,
cakewalk and jive,
ring shout and Lindy Hop,
Charleston and jitterbug
their sorrows away.

Like waves crashing ashore
and raindrops forming a pool,

the people held hands
and raised their voices in song.

In churches and mosques,
temples and healing places,
the people laid their troubles down

like a woven and embroidered rug,
a tapestry of memories and sorrow,

and a prayer for unknown tomorrows.

The people remember
that they have a job,
they have a duty.

UJIMA.

Collective work and responsibility.

The people remember
that freedom had a price.

With forty acres and a mule,
a bale of cotton and a bushel of rice,

with a silver dollar
and a nugget of gold,
and all the fruits and vegetables
a wooden cart could hold,

the people gathered their wealth
like raindrops in a storm cloud
and plowed the land
to sow a farm,

purchased wood
to build a store,
paved a road
to establish a town.

From Rosewood, Florida,
to Greenwood, Oklahoma;
from Africatown, Alabama,
to Freedman's Village, Virginia;

the people carved out a slice
of this American pie
and had themselves
a fine dessert.

Sojourner Truth told the people,
I sell the shadow to support the substance.

Marcus Garvey's Black Star Line
brought some of the people back to Africa.
This long journey home—
a sweet, sweet justice.

Madam C. J. Walker
became a millionaire
when she said to the people,
Love your hair!

Garrett A. Morgan
and George Washington Carver
invented all the new and different ways
the sun could shine—
bright or dim, hot or cool.
Like a bountiful farm
with finely tilled soil,
and a well-oiled city
with all its traffic lights
turned green,

the people's wealth
grew and grew,
and it rained freedom.

UJAMAA.

Cooperative economics.

But the people remember
that it happened again and again.

It was on a day and on a night,
during winter, spring, summer, and fall,
while celebrating a wedding
and embracing a new baby,
while sending a loved one
to distant shores

fighting that other great big war,
and while guarding a home
from the unwelcoming presence
of white-hooded strangers.

The people remember
that it happened again and again.

From Birmingham to Little Rock,
Selma to Memphis,

the people grew weary of
the low-hanging strange fruit—
lynched fathers and mothers,
sons and daughters—
cut from those mighty tree branches
that were like the arms of ancestors,
like the ships, like the ocean,
like the land itself.
Holding, bearing, and protecting.

The people remember
all those strange, bittersweet fruit
whose seeds were buried deep beneath
the earth to sprout, to bloom,
and to return home soon.

There on the streets,
with picket signs, arm in arm,
the people marched to lift every voice
and sang the songs of
a low-swinging sweet chariot.

Dr. King gathered the people
on that great big lawn
near that mighty white house
and shouted his dream
out to the sun
where it could be heard
even from the depths
of the great wide sea.

Change filled the air
when the people stood
one behind the other
on lines as long as history
to cast their vote,
this precious note
placed on ballots.

There on the sidewalks
of Harlem, the mecca of hope,
Malcolm X stood atop
his great wooden soapbox
and told the people to remember
by any means necessary,
lest they grow
more and more weary.

And the brothers and sisters,
with afros as round as the moon
and dashikis colorful like rainbows,
shouted out loud,
"I'm Black and I'm proud!"

With raised fists
to demand justice,
the people remember
that they have a
purpose.

NIA.

Even as Jim Crow's dogs
waged war on the people's bodies
and firehoses threatened
to wipe them out,
the people rose up
again and again, in every city,
as Martha and the Vandellas
sang "Dancing in the Street."

There was a new sound in town,
a drumbeat rhythm, a bass guitar,
a saxophone, and a trombone
pumping music, sweet music
out of Detroit, Michigan.

Motown told the people
to get down, get down.

A little boy named Michael
danced and sang his way
into the people's hearts
as he and his four brothers moved
like robots, like dancing machines.

Aretha, the soul queen,
demanded R-E-S-P-E-C-T
and told the people to rock steady,
as they steady rocked
to Jimi Hendrix's electric guitar,
and out of the sky fell the stars,

a constellation made of
Smokey and Stevie,
Diana and Nina,
whose Negro spirituals
became gospel,
became rhythm,
became blues.

As the mothers and fathers
sent their sons to yet another war,
the people remember peace
and daisies rained from way up high
as rainbows arched across the sky.

Marvin Gaye asked what's going on
and the people replied by painting this world
with blues
deeper than the ocean,
as they swayed to a new rhythm—
a funk, a disco, a hip-hop
born out of jazz,
born out of gumboot dance,
born out of djembe drums.

There was a new beat on the streets,
so Amiri Baraka, Sonia Sanchez,
Lucille Clifton, Nikki Giovanni,
and Maya Angelou

put pen to paper
and made their words dance.

Here was another chance
at freedom, at justice,
as the people remember
that still, like dust, they rise.

The poets and storytellers
wove together the pieces of fabric
handed down to them
by Langston, Zora, Richard, and Ralph
to make themselves a new patchwork quilt.

James, Toni, Alice, and Octavia
stitched new stories

so the people could remember
to go tell it on the mountain,
that a girl named Pecola wanted blue eyes,
a woman named Celie loved the color purple,
and that Dana could travel back in time.

But out of the rubble of grays and browns
was a bass so loud, a groove so smooth
that the people had to get down to the ground
on gray concrete, on brown cardboard
as the disc jockey scratched a vinyl record,
turning the beat upside down and down side up,
sideways, backward, and forward.

The people rapped the words
as they took apart the beat
to dance along the jagged breaks.

The Bronx was the place to be
as the walls and subway trains
became canvases for masterpieces.

The people remember
that the beat is from the heart
and out of the heart comes the finest art.

KUUMBA.

Creativity.

The people's music and dance,
art and stories, fashion and poetry
crossed boundaries and borders,
mountains and oceans,
valleys and hills,
shantytowns and villages.

From Tokyo to Johannesburg,
Paris to Rio, London to Moscow,
the people inspired the world.

A new president, Barack Obama, claimed a seat,
the most powerful in all the land.
He demanded change and took a stand
with Michelle, Sasha, and Malia by his side.
They were their ancestors' dreams, the people's pride.

But the people remember
that it happens again and again.

A boy and his toy;
a teenager on the phone;
friends coming home from a party;
a girl asking for the right way—
their breath and their light
taken in just one shot.

But the people still remember
that with each rising sun is a new day.

With each new year is a new dream;
a new seed of hope unearthed, dusted, and polished.

The people know
that there will be a time of peace.

The people will gather the pieces of fabric—
cut, torn, shredded, and made unrecognizable
by the storms of time—

to sew together a tapestry of
their stories,
one fine quilt,
a blanket for the children
to keep them warm, protected, and safe.

The people remember to always have *faith*.

IMANI.

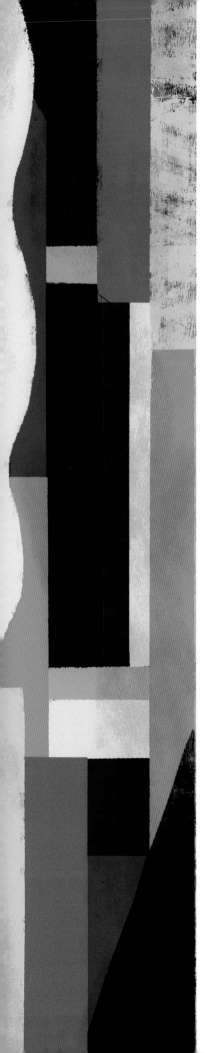

AUTHOR'S NOTE

I WAS BORN IN HAITI and immigrated to America as a child. My husband's parents are from Trinidad and Liberia and he was born in America—so our three children represent the African diaspora. They are Caribbean, West African, and African American. Celebrating Kwanzaa every year helps us to combine all these identities into one collective purpose.

Kwanzaa is celebrated for seven days starting December 25, on Christmas, through January 1, New Year's Day. First created in 1966 as a response to the many injustices faced by Black people in America and all over the world, Kwanzaa celebrates African American identity and purpose through its seven principles known as the Nguzo Saba. Kwanzaa is derived from the Swahili phrase "matunda ya kwanza," which means "first fruits," and Nguzo Saba, the "seven pillars."

I first started celebrating Kwanzaa in college. My professors were part of the civil rights movement and had witnessed some of the terrible racial violence that took place in our country in the sixties and seventies. Many of them recognized the need for Black people to create a collective identity and a sense of purpose through a yearly celebration. When I learned the seven principles of Kwanzaa and their meanings, they helped me find connection to my own ancestral history. I continued to celebrate Kwanzaa with friends, and, when I became a mother, I shared the principles with my family.

Before the first day of Kwanzaa, we set up the candleholder, or the kinara. There are seven candles, or mishumaa saba, one for each principle: Three red ones, three green ones, and one black one in the center to represent the first principle, Umoja, meaning "unity." The kinara is placed on a mat called the mkeka along with a cup of water called the unity cup, or kikombe cha umoja. A bowl of fruits and vegetables represents the crops during harvest, or the mazao. There are ears of corn, muhindi, to represent the children in the family. This is the Kwanzaa altar. There are also gifts set on or around the altar to share with members of the family, especially the children, on each day of Kwanzaa. These gifts are called zawadi.

On each day of Kwanzaa, we greet each other by asking, "Habari gani?," which means "What's the news?" in Swahili. We respond with the principle for that day. For example, on December 25, if I ask you, "Habari gani?," you respond by saying, "Umoja!"

Each principle is paired with an affirmation, and on every day of Kwanzaa, a candle is lit, starting with the black one for unity, while both the principle and its meaning are recited. We alternate between the red and green candles for each principle:

UMOJA (oo-MOE-jah) - *Unity*: To strive for and maintain unity in the family, community, nation, and race.

KUJICHAGULIA (koo-jee-chagoo-LEE-ah) - *Self-determination*: To define ourselves, name ourselves, create for ourselves, and speak for ourselves.

UJIMA (oo-JEE-mah) - *Collective work and responsibility*: To build and maintain our community together and make our brothers' and sisters' problems our problems and solve them together.

UJAMAA (oo-JAH-mah) - *Cooperative economics*: To build and maintain our own stores, shops, and other businesses and to benefit from their profits together.

NIA (nee-AH) - *Purpose*: To make our collective vocation the building and development of our community in order to restore our people to their traditional greatness.

KUUMBA (koo-OOM-bah) - *Creativity*: To always do as much as we can, however we can, in order to leave our community more beautiful and beneficial than we inherited it.

IMANI (ee-MAH-nee) - *Faith*: To believe with all our heart in our people, our parents, our teachers, our leaders, and the righteousness and victory of our struggle.

KWANZAA is also a time to honor history and to remember the sacrifices of those who came before us. On each day of Kwanzaa, I read books with my family and friends; however, I've always wanted there to be one book that both celebrates the principles of Kwanzaa and tells the story of Africans in America as a lyrical narrative, like a song or long poem that can be shared throughout the year, and every year. This is how the idea for *The People Remember* was born.

The People Remember tells the journey of African descendants in America. It begins in Africa, where families were torn apart during the transatlantic slave trade. I call this a time of war. People from different parts of West Africa were taken from their homes and families. They belonged to villages and communities and some from entire nations such as the Yoruba people and the Ashanti people. These Africans spoke different languages and had different customs. Yet, they were bound and chained and forced onto ships sailing to the New World, where they formed bonds that enabled them to work together and fight for their freedom. All these people from different African nations had to learn one common language and create a culture that combined their memories of home in Africa with new traditions that allowed them to survive and thrive. *The People Remember* is about survival as well as the many moments of joy, celebration, and innovation.

TIMELINE OF EVENTS

1518–1853
THE TRANSATLANTIC SLAVE TRADE

The transatlantic slave trade is one of the greatest atrocities in the world's history. Millions of Africans were captured and sold to Europeans from Portugal, Great Britain, France, and Spain. African people had their own customs and traditions, and many belonged to independent nation states. Those who were kidnapped and enslaved had to adapt to the customs of the Europeans and faced harsh treatment in the New World—the Americas, which included Brazil, North and South America, and the Caribbean. The first ship carrying enslaved Africans arrived in America in 1619 along the shores of Jamestown, Virginia. In 1808, the United States banned the importation of enslaved Africans; however, the illegal transportation of human cargo persisted and slavery continued to thrive. There were many uprisings and movements calling for the end of slavery around the world and in the United States, including the abolitionist movement, during which Sojourner Truth traveled across the country, selling her portraits to support the cause, and gave her most famous speech, "Ain't I A Woman." Harriet Tubman was an enslaved woman who led others to free states in the North through the Underground Railroad. Nat Turner led a rebellion in Virginia in 1831.

1861–65
THE AMERICAN CIVIL WAR

The American Civil War started because the states in the North and the states in the South disagreed on slavery, states' rights, and westward expansion. Eleven Southern states seceded and became known as the Confederacy. Black men volunteered to fight in the Civil War, and, in 1863, the government formed the Bureau of Colored Troops. On January 1 of that year, President Abraham Lincoln issued the Emancipation Proclamation declaring that all enslaved people in the Confederacy were now free. However, slavery continued in the Union states. It was not until December 18, 1865, when the Thirteenth Amendment was adopted into the Constitution that slavery was legally abolished in the United States.

1865–77
THE RECONSTRUCTION ERA

The Reconstruction era marked the end of the Civil War and the rebuilding and reunification of the states under one union. There were four million African Americans who were freed and had no resources to start their new lives. The government under President Andrew Johnson's leadership had to figure out how to integrate them into society.

Many African Americans traveled between states in search of loved ones who had been sold or had run away to Northern states. The Reconstruction Act of 1867 allowed Black people to be elected into the U.S. Congress—many of whom ran and won seats. The ratification of the Fourteenth Amendment granted freed Black men the right to vote.

1877–1916
SEPARATE BUT (UN)EQUAL

The United States was now faced with what Black scholars called "The Negro Problem." A book of the same title was edited by Booker T. Washington and included essays by W. E. B. Du Bois. They were two of the leading voices addressing the social status of Black Americans. Although they strongly disagreed on methods, Washington and Du Bois both believed that Black Americans should work toward establishing their own societies where they could build wealth despite the persistence of racial segregation in the form of Jim Crow laws. In 1896, *Plessy v. Ferguson* upheld the "separate but equal" doctrine that allowed states to legally separate Blacks and whites. Racial violence persisted under this law as whites suppressed the freedom of Black people.

1916–70
THE GREAT MIGRATION

Black people sought refuge from racial violence and segregation in the South and trailed to Northern cities in search of jobs and a better life. This was called the Great Migration, and it continued for several decades as the demand for racial equality heightened during the civil rights movement. Black men also enlisted and fought in the First and Second World Wars, including the Tuskegee Airmen, the first Black military aviators in the U.S. Army Air Corps. However, migrants from the South and veterans faced just as much racial discrimination and violence in Northern cities. Some neighborhoods in both the South and the North thrived because of Black-owned businesses, such as in the Greenwood District (known as "Black Wall Street"), in Tulsa, Oklahoma, and in Harlem in New York City, where the Harlem Renaissance took place. In other parts of the country, Black families who were able to afford homes in white neighborhoods faced discriminatory practices by mortgage lenders, forcing them to buy homes only in certain areas. This is known as redlining, which keeps home values in Black neighborhoods low and prevents Black homeowners from building wealth.

1950s–68
THE CIVIL RIGHTS MOVEMENT

In 1955, Rosa Parks refused to give up her seat to a white passenger on a bus in Montgomery, Alabama. She was arrested and taken into custody by the police, and this sparked a citywide bus boycott organized by Dr. King. The Montgomery bus boycott led to a number of protests across the country, especially following the murder of fourteen-year-old Emmett Till in August of that same year by white men in Money, Mississippi. Emmitt Till's murder and Rosa Parks's arrest marked the beginning of the civil rights movement, which advocated for voting rights, equality, and an end to segregation. The Voting Rights Act of 1965 prohibited racial discrimination in voting.

1965–89
THE BLACK POWER MOVEMENT

The assassinations of Malcolm X in 1965 and Martin Luther King Jr. in 1968 gave rise to politically charged Black expression in the form of literature, poetry, music, theater, fashion, and fine art. Black people aimed to make connections with decolonization movements in Africa as well as adopt aesthetics that instilled pride like afros, cornrows, and dashikis. This era in American history was called the Black Arts Movement. In 1966, Bobby Seale and Dr. Huey P. Newton founded the Black Panther Party for Self-Defense, and in just a few short years it gained a nationwide following. The organization is credited for starting the Free Breakfast for School Children Program. The Student Nonviolent Coordinating Committee (SNCC) was another organization that grew out of the civil rights movement, and as more racial violence continued to plague the United States, some members moved away from nonviolent protest and leaned toward the earlier teachings of Malcolm X, who advocated for self-defense. Stokely Carmichael (who later changed his name to Kwame Ture) first chanted the phrase "Black Power" during a 1966 march in Mississippi. "Black Power" became the rallying cry for activists who advocated for self-sufficiency through Black-owned bookstores, printing presses, and schools. This later became known as the Black Power movement, and it lasted through the 1970s, taking on different forms until 1989, when Black Panther Party cofounder Dr. Newton was killed. However, many of the political ideals of the Black Power movement continue today in other calls for change, especially the Black Lives Matter movement.

1977–PRESENT
THE HIP-HOP ERA

From the transatlantic slave trade through slavery and the Great Migration, Black people brought with them their culture, their family traditions, and their music. The drum was a major part of many African traditions; however, drums were outlawed in the South during slavery. Plantation owners feared that enslaved Black people would use the drums to communicate with one another. Still, Black people celebrated with music and dance by using their hands, feet, bodies, and voices as instruments. Song and movement traditions such as spirituals, the blues, the ring shout, and the cakewalk served as foundations for Black music and dance. Gospel and jazz birthed the Motown sound in the 1950s and '60s, just as funk and the poets of the Black Arts Movement birthed hip-hop in the late 1970s. Major cities in the United States such as New York, Chicago, and Detroit were recovering from years of civil unrest in the form of riots following the death of Dr. King. Unemployment and poverty led to high crime rates and violence in these cities. But even in the midst of disenfranchisement, children were continuing to celebrate life through music and dance. One form of music evolved out of mixing vinyl disco records on a turntable to create a break beat. Someone would rap over that break beat, and this is how hip-hop was born in the South Bronx neighborhood of New York City. The Hip-Hop Movement continues to be the voice of young people all over the world.

2008–16
THE FIRST BLACK PRESIDENT

In 2008, Barack Hussein Obama became the first Black president of the United States. This historic moment instilled a sense of great pride for Black people all over the world. Michelle Obama, a prominent lawyer, became the first Black first lady and together with their daughters, Sasha and Malia Obama, they resided in the White House for two terms, or eight years.

2012–PRESENT
THE BLACK LIVES MATTER MOVEMENT

In July 2012, seventeen-year-old Trayvon Martin was shot and killed in Florida by George Zimmerman, who claimed to be acting as a member of a community watch group. Zimmerman was acquitted of all charges the following year, which led to a wave of protests across the country. Many people also expressed outrage on social media, notably Patrisse Cullors, Opal Tometi, and Alicia Garza, who used the hashtag #BlackLivesMatter. This hashtag became a national movement when Cullors, Tometi, and Garza turned it into an organization of activists who strategize locally within a nonhierarchical structure—meaning there aren't any Black Lives Matter leaders. As racial violence continues to occur in big cities and small towns all over the United States, including the murders of Michael Brown, Tamir Rice, and Eric Garner, the rallying cry for protests in the streets and on social media continues to be Black Lives Matter. In 2020, in the midst of a global pandemic and as a response to the murders of George Floyd and Breonna Taylor, protesters continued to march, artists continued to make music, writers and poets continued to speak truth to power, and more and more children began to learn about the history, the resilience, the brilliance, and the importance of all Black lives.

FURTHER READING

Alexander, Kwame. *The Undefeated*. Illustrated by Kadir Nelson. New York: Versify, 2019.

Angaza, Maitefa. *Kwanzaa: From Holiday to Every Day*. New York: Dafina Books, 2007.

Giovanni, Nikki, ed. *Hip Hop Speaks to Children: A Celebration of Poetry with a Beat*. Naperville, IL: Sourcebooks, 2008.

Grifalconi, Ann. *The Village That Vanished*. Illustrated by Kadir Nelson. New York: Dial Press, 1656.

Hamilton, Virgina. *The People Could Fly: American Black Folktales*. Illustrated by Leo and Diane Dillon, PhD. New York: Alfred A. Knopf, 1985.

Medearis, Angela Shelf. *Seven Spools of Thread: A Kwaanza Story*. Illustrated by Daniel Minter. Park Ridge, IL: Albert Whitman & Company, 2000.

Myers, Walter Dean. *Harlem: A Poem*. Illustrated by Christopher Myers. New York: Scholastic Press, 1997.

Nelson, Kadir. *Heart and Soul: The Story of America and African Americans*. New York: Balzer + Bray, 2011.

Woodson, Jacqueline. *Show Way*. Illustrated by Hudson Talbott. New York: G.P. Putnam's Sons, 2005.

———. *This Is the Rope; A Story from the Great Migration*. Illustrated by James Ransome. New York: Puffin Books, 2013.